FATHERING YOUR SPECIAL CHILD

Books in the same series

A Special Book About Me
A Book for Children Diagnosed with Asperger Syndrome
Josie Santomauro
Illustrated by Carla Marino
ISBN 978 1 84310 655 5
Asperger Syndrome: After the Diagnosis series

You Are Special Too
A Book for Brothers and Sisters of Children Diagnosed with Asperger Syndrome
Josie Santomauro
Illustrated by Carla Marino
ISBN 978 1 84310 656 2
Asperger Syndrome: After the Diagnosis series

Mothering Your Special Child
A Book for Mothers or Carers of Children Diagnosed with Asperger Syndrome
Josie Santomauro
Illustrated by Carla Marino
ISBN 978 1 84310 657 9
Asperger Syndrome: After the Diagnosis series

Your Special Grandchild
A Book for Grandparents of Children Diagnosed with Asperger Syndrome
Josie Santomauro
Illustrated by Carla Marino
ISBN 978 1 84310 659 3
Asperger Syndrome: After the Diagnosis series

Your Special Student
A Book for Educators of Children Diagnosed with Asperger Syndrome
Josie Santomauro and Margaret-Anne Carter
Illustrated by Carla Marino
ISBN 978 1 84310 660 9
Asperger Syndrome: After the Diagnosis series

Your Special Friend
A Book for Peers of Children Diagnosed with Asperger Syndrome
Josie Santomauro
Illustrated by Carla Marino
ISBN 978 1 84310 661 6
Asperger Syndrome: After the Diagnosis series

Fathering Your Special Child

A Book for Fathers or Carers of Children Diagnosed with Asperger Syndrome

JOSIE SANTOMAURO

Illustrated by Carla Marino

Jessica Kingsley Publishers
London and Philadelphia

First published in 2009
by Jessica Kingsley Publishers
116 Pentonville Road
London N1 9JB, UK
and
400 Market Street, Suite 400
Philadelphia, PA 19106, USA

www.jkp.com

Library of Congress Cataloging in Publication Data
Santomauro, J. (Josie)
   Fathering your special child : a book for fathers or carers of children diagnosed with
asperger syndrome / Josie Santomauro ; illustrated by Carla Marino.
      p. cm.
   ISBN 978-1-84310-658-6 (pb : alk. paper) 1. Asperger's syndrome--Popular works.
2. Asperger's syndrome--Patients--Family relationships. 3. Parents of autistic children. 4.
Caregivers. 5. Fathers. I. Marino, Carla. II. Title.
   RJ506.A9S36 2009
   618.92'858832--dc22
                                                     2008041356

British Library Cataloguing in Publication Data
A CIP catalogue record for this book is available from the British Library

ISBN 978 1 84310 658 6

Printed and bound in Great Britain by
Athenaeum Press, Gateshead, Tyne and Wear

To all fathers
You are a hero to your son
And a king to your daughter

I wish to thank all the wonderful
contributors who have given
permission to reprint their gifts of
poetry, reflections, writings and
private thoughts here in this
book.

Contents

Introduction

I congratulate you on reaching this point, to move on from the initial diagnosis of your child having Asperger Syndrome.

Your child may have been given the diagnosis of Asperger Syndrome by a pediatrician, psychologist, speech therapist, teacher or friend.

Diagnosis is the first hurdle and there will be many more hurdles in your child's life. The end result is the satisfaction that you were there for your child along the way. Friends, doctors, teachers will come and go, but you will be the stability in their life, and you will have made a difference. Your role is not only to help your child understand and accept their diagnosis, but to help people around your child to understand and accept their differences.

Although Asperger Syndrome may appear to consume your life sometimes, we try not to dwell on the negatives, but embrace the positives and your child's successes. Both parents can provide support to a child with Asperger Syndrome. While your role may be different to the female caregiver's, it's equally important and valuable to the child. In later years, this earlier support and involvement with your child will bear fruit, showing as a fuller, more complete relationship between father and child.

When my son was first diagnosed, little was known about Asperger Syndrome, particularly for parents. The aim of this book is to introduce Asperger Syndrome to you in a positive light, and to guide you, the father/male caregiver, through some issues that you may face on the Asperger Syndrome journey with your child.

My son, Damian, was diagnosed 13 years ago, at the age of five, therefore I am able to share my first-hand experiences. We can learn from those who have already started this journey as I have learned from others also. I encourage you to research and learn as much about Asperger Syndrome as you can, to equip yourself with the tools to support your child.

Based on personal experience I had found that some fathers didn't want to make a fuss about their child's diagnosis, or to create discord amongst the family/extended family. I'm not here to say we should be screaming the diagnosis from the roof-tops, I'm suggesting that the more information you gather, the more coping skills you will have to help you and your family deal with your child with Asperger Syndrome.

What is Asperger Syndrome?

There are various ways of defining Asperger Syndrome. I can only offer you basic information on the diagnostic area, but a wealth of information based on my experiences. I encourage you to seek further information from specialists, support groups, other parents, the internet and other resources. Knowledge is power – I can't state this enough. The more you learn, the more adept you will become in handling your child's journey.

Throughout this book you will find Asperger Syndrome referred to as AS, and sometimes as ASD. ASD is an abbreviation for autism spectrum disorder. Asperger Syndrome falls within the autistic spectrum.

On first meeting someone we make a number of judgements. We can tell their age and a lot about their character from their appearance, and we can tell from facial expressions and tone of voice what mood they are in. This enables us to react to them in an appropriate way.

People with AS don't find it so easy to recognize this information, and because they find eye contact difficult it is hard for them to interact easily with other people.

However, once they are diagnosed with AS, these difficulties can be understood and dealt with, and the benefits of AS can be appreciated.

What's wrong with my child?

Your child needs extra assistance in these four areas:

1. Social skills

2. Communication

3. Behaviour

4. Sensory stimulation.

Social skills

Two-way social interaction may be impaired due to the inability of your child to understand the rules of social behaviour. There may be little or no eye contact used when listening or speaking. A lack of empathy may be shown to others and others' interests/activities, unless they are of specific interest to your child.

Communication

Your child may speak at the appropriate age, but sometimes speech can be delayed. Speech may be pedantic and/or repetitive. Usually there are comprehension difficulties with verbal instructions etc. He/she tends to be a very visual thinker and learner.

Behaviour

Your child may become obsessive about particular possessions or objects. Preferring life to be predictable they don't cope well with change in situations, structure or routine. They may not cope well with verbal instructions, therefore to avoid negative feedback they may become defiant in their behaviour.

Sensory stimulation

Your child may have difficulty focusing attention due to hyper- or hypo-sensory input in the environment (e.g. they may need headphones in noisy places). They may need sensory experiences built into the day (e.g. stress balls or other fidget items).

Common features of Asperger Syndrome

A nger and frustration

S tress and anxiety

P roblems with speech and language

E asily distracted

R eality/Fiction confusion

G ross motor skills

E ccentric or odd behaviours

R igid and resistant to change

S ocial skills deficit

Y our child may be intelligent

N o or little eye contact

D oesn't like loud noises and crowds

R ote memory strong

O bsessional interests

M aking friends may be difficult

E mpathy – lack of

Let's take a closer look at Asperger Syndrome
Anger and frustration

- Your child may have temper tantrums or anger outbursts.

- They might find it hard to ask for help when feeling confused or frustrated.

Stress and anxiety

- They don't cope well with being teased or bullied.

- They are sometimes anxious over changes.

- They are often very stressed at school.

- They don't cope well with criticism or failure.

Problems with speech and language

- They may not realize that their voice is too loud.

- They may have a monotone voice or an unusual accent.

- They may require some speech therapy.

- They may have difficulty explaining what they want to say.

Easily distracted

- Maybe their room and school desk is untidy.

- They may have short-term memory problems.

- It can be hard for them to pay attention or focus.

Reality/Fiction confusion

- Sometimes they don't understand jokes or stories.

- They may believe that their dreams are real.

- They take things literally, such as 'pull your socks up', and don't understand sarcasm.

Gross motor skills

- They may appear clumsy or have an odd gait.

- They may have poor co-ordination and find some sports (especially ball games) challenging.

Eccentric or odd behaviours

- They may have eccentric/odd behaviours.

- They may have eccentric/odd collections/hobbies.

Rigid and resistant to change

- They prefer routine and structure.

- They work best when forewarned about events.

- They may not work well with transitions.

Social skills deficit

- They may find it hard to understand people's body language.

- They need help to ignore teasing and bullying.

- They may be unaware of social rules and can sometimes appear rude.

Your child may be intelligent

- They can be very intelligent – especially at maths, science and computers.

- They are nicknamed 'little professor' by some professionals.

No or little eye contact

- They don't like looking into people's eyes when they talk to them and may look at the ground instead of someone's face.

- They may find the ground more interesting than your face but they are still listening to what you are saying.

Doesn't like loud noises and crowds

- They are sensitive to sensory stimuli.

- Noisy or crowded places, like shopping centres or parties, can overload their sensory system.

Rote memory strong

- Excellent long-term memory.

- Walking encyclopedia for specific facts.

Obsessional interests

- An obsession with a particular hobby/subject can dominate conversations, play and daily life.

- Repetitive movements, e.g. flapping their hands, touching their face or blinking.

Making friends may be difficult

- They might not have many friends and find it hard to make new friends.

- They may not have a desire to have friends, they may prefer to be on their own.

- They may prefer to play with older or younger people.

Empathy

- Sometimes they can't understand how other people are feeling.

- They may find it difficult to understand facial expressions.

Here's another acrostic to show some other characteristics of Asperger Syndrome:

A rtistic	**S** ignificant
S mart	**Y** why? Asks lots of questions
P unctual	**N** atural
E ngaging	**D** etermined
R epetitive movements	**R** esourceful
G ood natured	**O** ver sensitive
E xtraordinary	**M** aths wiz
R ules	**E** motional

Good Grief

When a parent is told their child has a disability they need to go through the classic stages of grief.

Grief is the natural healing process of a loss. You as a father may also grieve the news of your child's diagnosis. You may also be crucial to helping the mother in her grieving period. Allow family members to grieve. It's healthy to grieve. It's a health hazard to bury emotions.

Grief comes with a sense of loss, of a loved one, a job, pet, home or physical action. Even aging can cause grief. So the grief experienced at the loss of the 'normality' of a child can have the same impact as these other losses. A diagnosis of a disability, disease or life-threatening illness can have a devastating effect on the whole family.

The diagnosis of a child with Asperger Syndrome can have the same impact on a family as news of a death.

The grieving process begins, and it is important that the family is allowed to grieve in their own way. Each person should take the necessary time to grieve, without pressure to 'pick themselves up'. It is very important that support is in place to assist the grieving process along.

These are some feelings/behaviours that you may experience:

- denial

- shock

- anger

- guilt

- regret
- depression
- loneliness.

There are many changes about to happen to the family of a newly diagnosed child. They will gradually learn to understand and accommodate these changes and move on to a different path.

The stages of grief are denial, anger, sadness and then, finally, acceptance.

Denial: The initial shock. It's difficult to believe what you've just been told. 'This can't be happening to us.'

Anger: The most difficult stage. 'It's not fair, why us?' This stage introduces feelings of guilt. 'What have we done to deserve this?' Self-blame may become a problem, or you may blame doctors, schools, etc. Your anger may also be directed at the child.

Sadness: The essential ingredient of the grieving process. Cry, cry and more crying, it's good for the process, don't hold back, don't swallow it.

Acceptance: Resuming life. Getting back to the way things were prior to diagnosis but on a different level. This is the sign that the grieving process is nearing the end.

It may take more than six months to grieve or it may take some years, but the process is essential. Blocking it or not allowing grief will only create problems later, e.g. breakdown/depression.

Friends and family may try to make you feel better by saying things like: 'It's not the end of the world'/'Life goes on'/'Be strong'. These aren't exactly the things you or your partner wants to hear at this time, but they mean well. Finding a friend or support group who will help and listen is very beneficial.

How did my child get Asperger Syndrome?

It may be genetic, it may be due to the mother contracting a virus whilst pregnant, or it may be that the child contracts a virus in their first year. The best specialists still don't really know the exact answer to this question. Research and studies are ongoing.

With my son, it could have been any or all three of the above.

1. I think there may be some family members with mild traits.

2. At 22 weeks pregnant, I contracted a virus and was hospitalized due to dehydration.

3. At 11 months, Damian contracted the measles virus (one month before he was due for the immunization). He was very sick, and it took him about two months to recover. When he did get better, he reverted to crawling.

Asperger Syndrome is not caught like a cold, that glass of wine does not cause it during pregnancy, and it's not because your child fell and hit their head. Some say it's possibly due to immunizations, some say there's a possible dietary factor. Until the day the discovery of the cause is officially announced, I believe we should just move on and deal with the symptoms.

What we do know is that there is at least one in every 150 people who has Asperger Syndrome and, most importantly, through communication with adults with Asperger Syndrome, we do know how to make their lives easier and we can gain a better understanding of their world.

Been There, Done That

Learning from those who have been there before (whether they be other parents or adults with ASD) can be empowering in knowledge as well as reassuring to those just beginning to find their feet. I have found that the words from adults with ASD are precious, and by listening you can be guided with our decision-making when confronted by situations with your own child.

Einstein and Newton 'had autism'

Albert Einstein and Isaac Newton may have suffered from a type of autism, according to experts.

Researchers at Cambridge and Oxford universities believe both scientists displayed signs of Asperger Syndrome. Many people with AS are regarded as being eccentric. They sometimes lack social skills, are obsessed with complex topics and can have problems communicating. This latest research suggests that Einstein, who devised the theory of relativity, and Newton, who devised the laws of gravity, had these traits to varying degrees.

According to the researchers, Einstein showed signs of AS from a young age. As a child he was a loner and often repeated sentences obsessively until he was seven years old. He was also a notoriously confusing lecturer. Later in life, the German-born scientist made intimate friends, had numerous affairs and spoke out on political issues.

However, the researchers insist that he continued to show signs of having AS. 'Passion, falling in love and standing up for justice are all perfectly compatible with Asperger Syndrome,' Professor Simon Baron-Cohen of Cambridge, one of those involved in the study, told *New Scientist* magazine. 'What most people with Asperger Syndrome find difficult is casual chatting – they can't do small talk.'

My life with Asperger

It is difficult to find the words to describe the effects of Asperger Syndrome, in order for people who are NT (Neurologically typical) to understand. The problem is that not being NT, I don't know what their experience is like. Of course, communication is a major problem for people with Asperger Syndrome.

Over the years, I have learned to cope with AS whilst not knowing I had it. I only found out in early 2000. I have forced myself to look people in the eye when I talk to them, as well as to take part in conversations with people whilst attempting to give the impression that I am empathetic. I can sympathize with people to a certain extent but I don't have direct access to my emotions. I sometimes use the wrong emotional response. I also cannot manage my facial expressions. If someone asks me to smile for instance, I can't, unless I have access to a mirror. Empathy just doesn't come naturally to me. I also have to keep a watch on my tendency to steer the conversation around to my interests all the time.

I have problems deciding when to start speaking in a conversation, so I tend to interrupt the other person constantly. If several people are having a conversation and attempt to include me, I find myself focusing so much that I can't keep up with the conversation. By the time I have thought of something to say the topic has usually moved on. My thinking seems to slow down and people start to look at me oddly. I recall one occasion where I was in a social situation and had been introduced to some friends of a friend of mine. They were all talking to me and my mind just sort of shut down, too much input I guess. I became incoherent and began rambling and I had to leave. This was just so embarrassing. I think that they thought I was on drugs!

With regards to my depression, I think that the reason I became depressed was lack of understanding from other people, including my parents and my brother. My brother in particular looked upon me as an embarrassment and would sometimes deny I was his brother at all.

As a teenager and when I was in my twenties I would spend hours analysing my relationships with others, trying to work out what I was doing wrong. I was constantly rejected, which severely affected my self-esteem.

It was not surprising that I became depressed. Yet when I suggested this as the cause of my depression I was told that this couldn't be the cause. How little did they know?

The anti-depressants helped a bit, along with some counselling, but the counsellor just didn't understand the way I viewed the world. I would patiently explain for instance that when I tried to relate to others it felt like a glass bell jar had been placed over me, cutting me off from other people. I just got blank looks or puzzlement.

I received various diagnoses, such as I was suffering from a number of personality disorders and neuroses. I always knew that they were wrong.

I felt like other people were a different species. As a child I even convinced myself that I was an alien as it was the only explanation which made sense to me at the time. I was convinced for years that my parents had adopted me, as I was so unlike them.

I am glad that I finally know that I really am different from others. I always knew that I was but no one took me seriously. I guess over the years I learnt how to deal with my problems to a certain extent. I have come a long way but still have a way to go.

Iain Payne (UK) Adult with Asperger Syndrome

Ian has also been disgnosed as having a number of
developmental disorders and anxiety)

Asperger never leaves

Asperger Syndrome if you have it never leaves, in actual fact it never gets better! There is no cure, but as we get older we learn new ways around corners.

Circumstances alter and we may be given advice in coping strategies and that is what it is, just coping. In the end, we devise methods of getting around those corners on our own. Sometimes we do it well, sometimes not, but anybody who lives in close contact knows that we have not really changed, but that we still have those problems.

It is only those people who are not close to us that can be fooled. The key words here being 'close to us', as we tend not to develop closeness with many people.

Rest assured that the day will never dawn when you will awaken to find ASD on any level gone.

Yes, your child will probably need help in mainstream school, and as he gets older will probably need more help, not less.

Nanna Shirl (Gin Gin, Australia)
'An old dyed in the wool – age early
seventies' with Asperger Syndrome

Change, Change and More Change

Change, change and more change
Of context, place and time.
Why is it that life's transient stage
Plays havoc with my mind?
You said, 'We'll go to McDonald's'
But this was just a thought.
I was set for hours,
But the plan then came to nought.
My tears and confused frustration,
At plans that do not appear,
Are painful beyond recognition
And push me deeper into fear.
How can life be so determined?
How can change be so complete?
With continuity there is no end.
Security and trust are sweet.
So, who said that change would not hurt me?
Who said my 'being' could not be safe?
Change said, 'You need continuity
In order to find your place'.
For change makes all things different,
They no longer are the same.
What was it that you really meant?
All I feel is the pain.

From the book *Life behind Glass*, a personal account of ASD
by Wendy Lawson (Southern Cross University Press,
Lismore, and NSW, Australia)

When I was younger I always knew that I was different

As a young person diagnosed with Asperger Syndrome, I find it increasingly difficult for non-autistic people to understand what Asperger Syndrome is. It would be like someone I didn't know coming up to me and saying that they have a disability which is unknown to me. I think that more awareness of the condition is happening but it can be frustrating when you are in your late twenties as I am. I think all people who have been diagnosed much earlier have the benefits of less hassles. Some people may choose to agree or disagree with me. At my age I find it difficult, as for all the years that I was undiagnosed, I knew nothing about Asperger Syndrome nor did anyone else. I find that as a seed that has existed frozen in time for all those years, it is a lot of work to catch up with my peers who are all married, have partners or who are working.

I am beginning to realize the conventions, for at my age not many young non-autistic people want to make friends, and I keep telling myself that this is the way it is. I have always found talking to myself the best solution to overcome this problem. I tell myself that I need to understand people and why I don't fit in.

When I was younger I always knew that I was different. I look back on my schooling years and don't have happy memories of either high school or primary school.

I think sometimes that those with Asperger Syndrome have been specially chosen to carry the goodness on this earth.

Garry Burge (Brisbane, Australia)
Adult with Asperger Syndrome

Our personal experience

Six years ago, my son was diagnosed at age nine with mild Asperger Syndrome. He had experienced extreme school anxiety and depression as well as some phobias. He has come a long way in working his way through these obstacles. I would like to share some of my observations from our journey.

I have noticed the frustration and guilt that parents often go through in trying to sift through all the different choices that come before them. We agonized over whether to send our child to school or to home school, whether to give him a particular medication, vaccination, food supplementation, special diet, method of discipline/therapy to use; the list goes on. Often, guilt over a past choice may linger if we see no improvement, or fear may arise if we are faced with new choices that we are unfamiliar with.

From my own personal experiences and observations over the years, I have come to realize that at each step, each individual family must make the choice that seems the best at that time.

As important as each choice may seem, there is an even more crucial factor than the choice itself – love. It sometimes can seem overwhelming when we list the pros and cons and feel that if we make the 'wrong' choice, our child loses time, or worse, remains lost forever. The most significant factor that I have ever witnessed in the positive growth and development of any child is the underlying support and encouragement of a loving family.

Whatever the choice at whatever particular stage, we should undertake it with gentleness and love. That's the crucial ingredient. Whether we feel home schooling or a public school is best for our child at the moment is an individual decision. But whichever one we decide is best, it will be invalidated, or worse, a negative experience for all, if it is carried through grudgingly. The loving commitment and support that we transmit to our child is the key to opening the door.

In our own journey with our son we have come upon various 'difficult' choices concerning schooling, medication, counselling, therapies, etc. Sometimes we agreed with schools or psychiatrists, sometimes not. There were often 'advantages' of a path we didn't choose to take – yet we felt at that time that a different path was more comfortable, convenient or reasonable for our family situation as a whole…so many factors. We know that we need to be flexible enough to change a direction when we feel it is no longer useful. We also try to be open to ideas that we might not have considered before. We know not to get stuck in guilt or regret, but to learn from any mistakes and move on. Above all, we embrace the challenge of loving our son into becoming all that he can be.

Laura Gilbert (USA) Mother of a
teenager with Asperger Syndrome

The Journey

You are driving along a highway,
a caravan of cars — all friends.
Your plan is to stick to the main highway,
your destination is mapped out.
Your car is stopped by an official.
You aren't allowed to continue, you must detour,
turn off onto a dirt track.
'But my friends are on that highway, we're following each
other' you try to explain.
You are disorientated,
and don't want to take the dirt track.
But there's no turning back, the highway is closed to you,
you have no other choice.
The track is bumpy, windy,
and a much longer drive than what was originally planned
for.
You run out of petrol, have flat tyres
and engine failure many times.
You begin to resent your friends who are on the
highway,
why didn't they have to take the detour?
Why are they cruising along?
You eventually get to your destination
and find your friends.
You are now driving side by side in different lanes.
Their trip wasn't as bad as yours, they made it earlier,
but it wasn't without its disruptions either.
You have many stories to share
about your adventurous drive,
and in the end — it has made you a seasoned traveller!

Josie Santomauro

Raising my son with Asperger Syndrome

I have been totally involved in bringing up my only son. The problems started when he attended school, he being a very mild-natured boy, his classmates could make him do anything and he got into trouble. He could not copy from the blackboard. He could read and write but his handwriting was illegible. When he was in grade two he could not cope with the class routine. He was assessed by numerous specialists, who used words like IQ, MR and autism, I was not fully aware of my son's condition, nor what these labels meant.

I came to know of Asperger Syndrome upon reaching Chennai when my son was nearly 11 years old. Our consultant explained the condition of our son and gave reasons for hope. My son is very trusting and likes people, he will walk away with total strangers. Once he was missing for a good part of the day and finally when he was found at the home for destitutes, he was quite at ease playing there. He did not display any emotion at being lost or when we found him!

What can we do to help such children come up in life and earn their livelihood independently? They need help and support right through their lives, who will look after them after us, this worries me a lot. Any training that we parents can get will go a long way in rehabilitating these children, to my mind a conference or seminar should attempt to do just that.

Institution for Remedial Intervention
Services, Chennai, India, www.autismindia.com

One Hundred Tears

A hundred times I told him, a hundred times and more,
'Don't hit the dog, don't run away, don't throw
that on the floor!'

All morning he was busy, he didn't stop to think.
He broke my lamp and spilled his milk,
Dumped the kitten in the sink.

He ran around the house all day without
a stitch of clothes.
He flapped his hands and laughed and cried,
And fell and bumped his nose.

At dinner came the moment when I'd simply
had enough.
He dumped his dinner on the floor and that's
when I got tough.

I sent him off to bed right then, despite his tearful pleas.
I let him cry himself to sleep – it brought me
to my knees.

When silence fell upon his room I slowly crept inside,
And gazing on his tear-stained face I broke down
and I cried.

A hundred tears I wept that night,
A hundred tears and more,
For this little boy who spilled his milk on my nice
bright shiny floor.

Why am I to scold my son for things he cannot know?
He looks to me for patience to help him learn and grow.

A hundred prayers I said that night, a hundred prayers
and more
Help me Lord to teach my child this child that I adore.

And as I left his room that night, I kissed his tears away,
And promised that tomorrow would be a better day.

(For Dhylan)

Sally Meyer (USA)

What Now?

What happens once your child is diagnosed?

Generally a chain of events begins where there is a support system set up for your child. Schools may begin to look at the best way to support your child. You may begin to look at the best way of introducing different types of therapy to your child, such as speech therapy and social skills classes. You and your partner may also look at educating yourselves in the areas of behaviour management and positive parenting.

Not only will you have the above to contend with, but you will also have the general public, family and friends who may not understand or accept your child's behaviour as a form of disability. They may prefer to judge your child as naughty or spoiled or proceed to tell you that they 'need a good smack!'

Dealing with family, friends and the public

I used to defend my parenting skills vigilantly! I would be emotionally exhausted. I was trying to justify that my life wasn't as easy as theirs, continually justifying reasons for not attending family functions, etc. Yes, our lives do seem harder, but hey, why do we have to make a song and dance about it? If people are interested, they will ask. So I find now that I only speak about our problems/issues/good-news items regarding ASD and Damian if I'm asked. I have come to realize that the important thing is that we tell 'ourselves', and listen to 'ourselves'.

Dear Josie,

Do you have any insights into how to deal with the reactions of extended family and friends? I'm getting mixed responses. Some are supportive and some think it's bunk and that Kate (my partner) and I just need to parent better. I'm trying to educate and help them, but some things that are being said (and not said) are hurtful. I would like any advice if you have any.

Thanks, Mike

Hi Mike,

I used to try to do the same thing with educating, etc., but in the end you are running around in circles, ragged, and the people who question your skills seem to be fresh as daisies! The important primary issue is that you, your partner and your child (and any siblings) understand and accept the diagnosis. Who cares about the others – at this stage, anyhow? You have to be very firm and take a stand together as partners, especially when family members make comments regarding your parenting. Don't justify or defend your parenting skills, but keep repeating a phrase that you're comfortable with, e.g. 'He has a mild disability, and we are putting into place strategies to help him for his future.' You don't have to explain why, when, how, what or whatever! Be a broken record with your comment, repeat, repeat and repeat. They will eventually get the message that they can't say anything to change you, and one day they may start to show an interest, and that's the key time – when they are interested, it means that they will learn. There's no use trying to teach them now about the disability if they have 'shut-down'.

Don't let any hurtful comments in – put up an invisible shield and see them as scared and frightened people who don't want to accept any changes in 'their' lives. Just know what the truth is, and the truth is that you are doing the best for your child!

Hope this helps.

Josie

Awareness

Below is a sample card you can photocopy, cut out, fold in half and glue to carry in your wallet, or you can make up your own cards. This is a great way to create awareness of Asperger Syndrome to strangers and members of the public. Because your child may appear neurotypical members of the public sometimes believe that your child's challenging behaviour is due to behaviour management.

An example of when I used the card was when we were on public transport and Damian was tired, stressed and overwhelmed after a big day out. He wanted to get home and did not have the patience to sit on the bus. He therefore threw a public tantrum and verbally abused me. An elderly couple a few rows down whispered loudly that they thought he needed some discipline. As we approached our stop, I pulled out the card and handed it to them as we hopped off the bus.

Asperger Syndrome affects my child in their communication, behaviour and learning abilities. Therefore my child may experience difficulties in certain social situations. The result being sensory overloads which can sometimes lead to challenging behaviours. We appreciate your patience and understanding.	

Hints, ideas and strategies

- See their hobby/obsession as an advantage and use it when trying to put a point across, or when teaching them a strategy or as an incentive in a goal system. E.g. Damian was obsessed with Star Wars, so when we wanted him to be very interested in something we would use Star Wars characters as people or Star Wars computer games as a reward.

- Use language appropriate to your child's understanding – don't go 'over their head' with long descriptive sentences. Keep it short and sweet. E.g. if I asked Damian to do three chores, and instructed them all in a verbal row he would always hear only the first or the last chore. So now I either write it down for him, or just tell him one at a time.

- Don't all talk at once to the child. This can sound like a muffled room full of people at a party and can be very confusing for the child. It is a good idea for one person to speak at a time, turn taking so the child can listen and absorb the information.

- Use visual charts, timetables, rosters, etc. Damian had a morning and afternoon roster, so he could organize himself to and from school. This helped him become independent and in later years he did not require the visuals any longer as he could think for himself, he had learned it all by rote. When preparing a visual chart, timetable or roster, photographs of the child 'doing' are best, otherwise computer graphics are acceptable.

- When introducing a new activity or routine, draw a 'What do I do' visual story. E.g. in primary school Damian was to catch the school bus on his own. We drew up a visual story with step by step of what he was to do, and this also included some 'what ifs', e.g. what if the bus didn't come, etc. We made a large story about 'Catching the Bus', and also had one reduced down in size for him to keep in his school bag/pocket so he could refer to it. It was a huge success, and he became independent and could catch the bus home like other, neurotypical children.

- Set realistic, achievable goals for your child. When setting goals check whether they are achievable by your child, as every child's progress is different. Also does the main goal need to be broken down into smaller goals first before it can be achieved?

- Do not join the 'angry game'. When a situation is escalating, send your child to time out and walk away, have a cup of tea and wait at least half an hour for emotions to settle down before dealing with the problem. I find that if Damian comes home with a dark mood, I leave him alone for at least half an hour. He goes straight to his room, then when he has had downtime he emerges to talk to me. If I am in his face when I know that he is in a dark mood, then he will just become aggravated and take his day's frustrations out on me.

- If you feel that all is failing, please don't hesitate to ask for help, don't wait for issues to escalate and possibly get out of control. There are various avenues of help: Parent-line, support groups, school counsellor, etc. Do not think that asking for help is a sign of failure. It is a sign of strength to ask for help as you are looking at solutions and not burying your head in the sand.

- Play games with your child to encourage turn taking, etc. Some great games are simple board games and some card games.

- Listen to yourself – are you using positive talk? Sometimes we need to hear ourselves and others around us – are we speaking positively or negatively? If we expect these children to learn to be positive, then we need to model this behaviour.

- Eventually, parents will need to share the diagnosis with their child. They will know when they are both ready. Be supportive and patient. It is very important to wait until the child is ready. There is no use in giving information when it is not required, as this can sometimes overwhelm a child who previously thought there was nothing wrong or different. There will come a day, whether the child is eight or eighteen, when they will begin to question their difference.

- If you notice your child becoming distressed, you can remind them to take themselves to time out or a quiet area to wind down. Sometimes it is best to give them a wide berth to calm down – do not attempt to deal with a situation as it is happening unless there is an issue with safety. It's always a good idea to give them time to wind down.

- Remind your child to look at their charts and timetables. If you are aware that they are struggling with a challenge and they do have a chart/timetable with that scenario, a gentle prompt is beneficial to remind them they have visual cues to help.

- Remind them of any changes or new things that are going to happen, like birthdays or lessons. Sometimes we get so caught up in what is going to happen or preparing to go somewhere that we forget to inform the child that they are included. If they have a whiteboard calendar, talk to them about it and add it to the calendar. And a reminder the day before as well as on the day is helpful also.

- Warn your child about changes they don't know about. Changes are hard for children with AS, in particular if they were looking forward to going somewhere. It can be a huge let down as they have planned the scenario over and over in their heads. So if they were looking forward to seeing the real pirate at the pirate party and then you arrive and the pirate is not coming because he is sick, take the child to a quiet area and explain calmly what has happened. Sometimes we do not know how they will react. They may accept this information or they may be triggered into a tantrum. Use behavioural management strategies if the latter happens.

- Try to tell them all about where you are going or what is about to happen. Even draw a picture for them, or write down what you know. E.g. when Damian was to attend his first school camp we went for a drive and took him to the grounds, walked around, showed him the rooms, where they would eat, etc. He also took photos and showed his class that week. We glued the photos to a chart, so he could become familiar with the campgrounds. The result was a successful camp!

- Asperger Syndrome does not mean all doom and gloom – you can have a healthy relationship with your child. Children with Asperger Syndrome have a wonderful sense of humour. Laugh and have fun with them.

The School Scene

Once your child is diagnosed, the education system should begin to look at the best way to support your child.

Your child spends half of their waking hours in a schooling environment, therefore they are exposed to many different types of stimuli, social aspects, rules, etc. It would be a perfect world if every child had a wonderful day at school free from social injustice, anxieties and pressures. We must work hand in hand with schools and yet keep our professional boundaries as parents representing the rights of the child.

You will always find in your child's 12-year schooling journey that there will be the predators and the carers – in both teachers and peers. Helping your child to deal with the predators is arming them with tools for life.

You have many choices with the way your child is schooled; do not ever feel that you are locked into one type of schooling. Do your research, as well as speak with other parents. Schools who do cater for our children build up a reputation amongst support groups. Alternatively, you may choose to home school your child.

Conflicts between parents and schools can arise, which sadly can become barriers to your child's best interests. To help you overcome the barriers:

- Learn more about special education and your child's rights.

- Ask for a mediator to attend all meetings if you feel it's required.

- Keep a written record of all meetings and conversations held.

Your child's IEP (Individual Evaluation Plan)

Once your child is officially diagnosed, you may find that the school then introduces an IEP. Basically this is a support system for your child where the support team at school can monitor your child's progress as well as teach your child and his/her teacher strategies to cope with their day.

The usual process with an IEP is for the team, consisting of teacher, support teacher, aide, parent and others, to meet. At this meeting, goals are set that are specifically catered to your child's needs. The goals are then monitored.

Each state and country has a different system. So it is worthwhile educating yourself about the IEP (or equivalent) in your area and what your child's rights are in regards to it.

A team cannot work without co-operation from all players, therefore you, being the key player, must co-operate with the school. If they require documentation from your child's medical team, or they require further testing to be done for your child, please assist them with this process. If the school recommends you attend parenting courses, don't be offended, they may be trying to achieve an all-round positive result for your child. The school representatives may be attending many courses in educating themselves to assist your child.

P reparation

R omance – the teacher/parent partnership

O ngoing

G oals for the IEP

R oles

A nger: Why are parents angry?

M eetings

Preparation

- Before attending meetings you should prepare by collecting thoughts on the goals/ questions/etc., relating to your child's IEP.

Romance – the teacher/parent partnership

- IEP meetings are famous for their awkwardness and tension.

- Regard the meeting as a negotiation within a partnership and not a standoff or a fight.

- During the meeting, take notes, listen carefully, make eye contact, use a gentle tone in your voice, don't make assumptions, and ask for clarification.

- Be assertive, not aggressive, don't take comments personally, and the end result should be a win–win situation, for all parties in the partnership.

- *Most importantly, it's about your child.*

Ongoing

- It may seem like an ongoing saga! But if you see it as a saga, you'll feel drained. See it as a positive experience and you'll feel rejuvenated by the accomplishments, even small ones, made by your child due to your positive approach to your child's IEP and goals.

Goals for the IEP

- Write down some goals that you think might benefit your child and bring them to the meeting.

- Ensure that the goals the school is considering are achievable by your child.

- Goals can range from improving social skills via group game sessions to improving your child's language/comprehension skills via modifying their schoolwork to suit their needs.

Roles

- Your paraprofessional role of parent is as important as other professionals and without each others' support the team can break down.

- The Education Department is responsible for the education of the child with ASD and is accountable to the IEP.

- The parent (who knows the child better than anybody!) is the key communicator and mediator between child and school.

- Very often the roles are reversed or totally confused. This is where people involved should be regarded as the 'team' and each player has a role. The main player is the parent but (at school) the captain is the classroom teacher, who can call for help or direct instructions from his/her support team.

Anger: Why are parents angry?

- When major changes to the IEP or goals are made without giving parents input.

- When the team, not knowledgeable about the situation at hand, automatically backs the teacher.

- Lack of following through/breaking promises.

- When the child is disciplined because of circumstances that have arisen due to the child's disability.

- About any problem or potential threat to the child.

- In general, 'failure to communicate'.

Meetings

- Adopt a professional approach to meetings.

- If you do not understand something, ask for clarification. Don't sit there and think that just because you didn't understand something, you're stupid and therefore don't want everyone else to think this! Stupid is sitting there and pretending you understand!

- Sometimes the meeting may overwhelm you. Write everything down, or ask permission to record the meeting on tape, so you can listen to the tape back at home.

Sacred Support

Although the journey will be made mostly with immediate family, it's important to have others who you can rely on, talk with or to be there to listen to you. Trying to do this with friends or family who don't fully understand your situation is sometimes hard. This is when support groups can be called upon.

Meeting other parents (in particular fathers) with ASD children is like meeting people who have a similar cultural background to you. They understand our language, our needs, our emotional roller coaster rides, our difficulties within society and most importantly, they understand our children.

Josie's journal

2 September 1995

Today was Damian's first session of 'Kids Club' with six other kids with AS and two teachers teaching them social skills. It was the first time we had seen other kids with AS. I sat down and couldn't help staring at them, and yet I felt comfortable looking at them. But I felt a big lump in my throat looking at Damian amongst these children – my Damian. I think Damian's father felt the same, we're obviously still grieving. And yet, I felt more at ease today because seeing what the other kids looked like (and acted like) confirmed within my own mind that Damian was like them and we have now reached help! During the kids session, the parents went to have coffee and I introduced Damian's father to another father who I knew to be an engineer and they hit it off – it was great.

Support groups

Individual support groups may operate differently to each other, but these are the basic aims of an Asperger Syndrome support group:

- to provide support to families and the individual with AS

- to provide information on Asperger Syndrome to parents and professionals

- to provide a resource library which includes books, videos, etc.

- to educate the community on Asperger Syndrome

- to organize workshops, seminars and guest speakers.

You can also visit the following very informative and helpful websites:

MAAP Services for Autism and Asperger Syndrome – a non-profit organization providing information to families of individuals with autism, AS and pervasive developmental disorder.
www.asperger.org

National Autistic Society, UK – provides help, support and services to individuals with autism and their families.
www.nas.org.uk

Dr Tony Attwood – the world-renowned clinical psychologist's guide for parents, professionals and people with AS and their partners.
www.tonyattwood.com.au

Asperger Services Australia – claiming to be the world's largest support group for AS, they provide support to parents, families, carers and siblings as well as to children, adolescents and adults with AS.
www.asperger.asn.au

Josie Santomauro – author and presenter on AS, Josie also writes children's fiction under the name Josie Montano.
www.booksbyjosie.com.au

OASIS – Online Asperger Syndrome Information and Support.
www.aspergersyndrome.org

The potential success of using a parent support group to meet the specific needs of parents with ASD children will depend to some extent on the following three classes of variables: child, parents and group leader. The findings of this two-part research project suggest that (a) parents feeling that their lot in life is similar to that of other group members and (b) parent perceptions of the level of their child's difficulties were important in prompting the feeling that support group participants had a common basis for communication and sharing of information. In addition, parents reported feeling most connected and understood by group leaders who possessed a high level of autism-specific knowledge and 'hands-on' experience in dealing with ASD children.

The present research compared the relative effectiveness of generalized counselling versus strategy-based parent support groups. Parents reported the most positive effects for the latter type of parent support group and this suggests that parents benefit from learning how to apply stress management strategies as well as being provided with the opportunity to communicate about the difficulties they face.

Christopher Sharpley, PhD, and Vicki Bitsika, PhD, MAPS Qld,
Behaviour Analysis & Consulting Services, Coolangatta,
QLD, Australia

Extract from conference paper titled 'Developing a support group which meets the specific needs of parents with children who have an autism spectrum disorder', originally presented at the 1999 National Autism Conference, Tasmania, Australia.

Looking after yourself

- Talk openly and honestly about any feelings you may have regarding your child with your partner.

- Seek out another father who shares similar experiences and you may discover a friendship.

- Make an effort once a week with your partner to treat yourselves with either dinner out, a massage or a movie.

- Combine healthy meals with exercise – keeping fit and healthy can help lift a low mood.

- Play uplifting music.

- Watch comedies to increase your endorphins.

- Read books about Asperger Syndrome.

- Studies show that women live longer than men because of their ability to express emotions freely…so forget the stiff upper lip and live longer!

- It's ok to show your sadness – researchers think that there is a male hormone that stops men from crying easily, so prove them wrong!

- Take your Superman cape off – you don't have to fix everything nor help everyone.

- Have some quiet time, no TV, no music, just silence or spend some time in nature.

- Accept help when it's offered to you.

- Express anger constructively, don't hold it in, either with a boxing bag, yelling in the car with the music up or going for a furious walk.

- Face your fears.
- To change takes great courage.

Moving from diagnosis to discovery

Unlike diagnosis, the term discovery often refers to the identification of a person's strengths or talents. Actors are discovered. Artists and musicians are discovered. A great friend is discovered. These people are identified by an informal combination of evaluation and awe that ultimately concludes that this person – more than most others – possesses admirable qualities, abilities, and/or talents. It's an acknowledgement that, 'you know, he's better than me at…'. In referring to people with respect to their talents or abilities, politically correct 'people first' terminology is not required; labels like musician, artist or poet are welcomed and considered complimentary.

If Asperger Syndrome was identified by observation of strengths and talents, it would no longer be in the DSM IV, nor would it be referred to as a syndrome. After all, a reference to someone with special strengths or talents does not use terms with negative connotations (it's artist and poet, not artistically arrogant or poetically preoccupied), nor does it attach someone's proper name to the word syndrome (it's vocalist or soloist, not Sinatra's Syndrome). Focusing on strengths requires shedding the former diagnostic term, Asperger Syndrome, for a new term. The authors feel that Aspie, used in self-reference by Liane Holliday Willey in her book, *Pretending to be Normal* (1999), is a term that seems right at home among its talent-based counterparts: soloist, genius, aspie, dancer.

The discovery of aspies brings into focus valuable, endangered opportunities that have repeatedly marched past without adequate notice of their potential. There is the opportunity to make new friends; a chance to consider those who may seem comparatively awkward, but decidedly more honest and genuine. In addition to discovering new friendships there is the opportunity to utilize unique perspectives and talents to tackle problems. There's work to do in the following century – diseases to cure, environments to save, freedoms to preserve. Fortunately, there are people with minds capable of the challenge, with the ability to focus and persevere. They possess perspectives and talents unique enough to solve the biggest of problems, or enhance the most challenging projects. They are aspies. They are living proof that the best places to play will always be those that are discovered.

Carol Gray (USA) and Tony Attwood (Australia), extracted from 'The Discovery of "Aspie": Criteria by Attwood and Gray' *Morning News, (a publication of Jenison Public Schools, Michigan) 11, 3 (Fall 1999).*

The End?

Of course it's not the end.

Unfortunately we tend to only hear the difficult and heart wrenching stories about having a child with Asperger Syndrome. Laura Gilbert shares with us her son's success story; she says, 'I believe that parents and children are mutual gifts to each other.' I believe she's right! It's all about how we perceive situations brought into our lives.

I have come to understand that it's whether you perceive the gift as a problem…or the problem as a gift…

Mutual Gifts

At 15, our son is now a very articulate, witty and socially aware adolescent. After all the counselling that he has had, covering the range from psychological self-help strategies to social skill development, in many ways he is now actually more sophisticated in understanding himself and others than many of his peers.

He now has a circle of friends that he developed on his own, makes honour roll every marking period, and requires no medication nor special help in school. He has never loved school, but functions well within the school environment and often with a sense of humour.

Since art is his forte and his passion, we tell him to be patient until the day that he can devote most of his time doing what he loves.

As with all of us, our son is still a 'work in progress'. But I've come to realize that through his fears, phobias and social misperceptions, I have learned and grown and become more than I ever was before. I believe that parents and children are mutual gifts to each other. We are given, in this life, exactly what we need to become all that we are truly meant to be.

Laura Gilbert (USA) Mother
of a teenager with Asperger Syndrome

I am…

I am the little engine that did.

When on my journey in life, my tracks led me to a mountain – a diagnosis of Asperger Syndrome – I looked at it with defeat – thinking there was no way I could climb over it. Then I pondered the obstacle before me, and then I said to myself over and over, 'I think I can, I think I can…', then I slowly started climbing the mountain saying to myself over and over, 'I know I can, I know I can', and then I made it over that ominous diagnosis of Asperger Syndrome and continued my journey. I am the little engine that did.

I am more devoted than Noah's wife.

I sometimes feel overwhelmed in my 'house-boat'…365 days and 365 nights a year, constantly working with and teaching my child. But when the storms of isolation and monotony become most unbearable, I do not jump ship. Instead I wait for the rainbow that is sure to come.

I am Xena.

Real life warrior goddess of Asperger Syndrome. With my steel-plated armour I can battle anyone who gets in the way of progress for my child. I can overcome the stares and ignorance of those without a disability in their lives – and educate them as to why my child is the way he is, and why he does the things he does.

With my sword of persistence, I can battle the schools to have them properly educate my child. Yes, I am Xena – and I am prepared for any battle that might come my way.

I am beautiful.

I have hairy legs because I get no time alone in the bathroom, and bags under my eyes from staying up all night with my child. The only exercise I get is the spring from my house to my car – to take my child to therapy. Dressed up to me is, well – just that I had a moment to get dressed! They say that beauty is in the eye of the beholder – and so even on the days when I don't feel very beautiful I will know that I am…because God is my beholder.

I am Bionic Woman.

With my bionic vision I can see through the disability my child has, and see the beauty in his soul and the intelligence in his eyes – when others can't. I have bionic hearing and can look at my child when he smiles at me, and hear his voice say, 'I love you Mummy,' – even though he can't talk. Yes, I am thankful to be bionic.

I am Mary.

A not so well known mother of a child with Asperger Syndrome who was brought here to touch the souls of those around him, in a way that will forever change them. And it started with me. By teaching me things I would never have known, by bringing me friendships I never would have had, and by opening my eyes as to what really matters in life. Things like the Joy of just living in the moment, the Peace of knowing that God is in control, never losing Hope, and knowing an unconditional Love that words cannot express. Yes, I too am blessed by a special child, just like Mary.

I am Superwoman.

I am able to leap over tall loads of laundry in a single bound, and run faster than a speeding bullet, to rescue my child from danger. Oh yes, without a doubt, I am Superwoman.

I am Moses.

I was chosen to be a mother of a child with Asperger Syndrome. I may at times question whether I am the right 'man' for the job…but God will give me the faith I need to lead my child to be the best he can be. And like Moses, God will give me the small miracles here and there, needed to accomplish my mission.

I am Stretch Armstrong.

A mum that can be stretched beyond belief – and still somehow return to normal. I can stretch limited funds to cover every treatment and therapy that insurance won't. I can stretch my patience as I bounce from doctor to doctor in a quest to treat my child. I can stretch what time I have, and share it with my husband, my children, and my church and still have some leftover to help my friends. Yes, my name is Stretch. And I have the stretch marks to prove it!

I am Rosa Parks.

I refuse to move or waver in what I believe is right for my child…simply because my view is the minority, not the majority. I refuse to believe 'What can one mother do?' But instead, I will write, call, and rally to the government if I have to, and do whatever it takes to prevent discrimination against my child and ensure that he gets the services he needs.

I am Hercules.

The Greek god known for strength and courage. The heavy loads I must carry would make others crumble to the ground. The weight of Sorrow, Fear at uncertainty of the future, Injustice at having no answers, and from Tears of despair, would alone possibly be too much, even for Hercules. But then the Joy, Laughter, Smiles, and Tears of pride – at my child's accomplishments – balance the load to make it easy to bear.

I am touched by an Angel.

An Angel who lives in a world of his own. And it's true. He lives in a world of innocence and purity. A world without hatred or deceit. A world where everyone is beautiful and where no one is ugly. A world where there is always enough time. A world where he goes to bed with no worries of tomorrow and wakes up with no regrets of the past. Yes, I most certainly am touched by an Angel, and in some ways his world is better…

I am a true 'Survivor' – the mum of a child, who has faced, is facing, and will face…some of the most difficult challenges life has to offer. I am ready for the challenge and have God given endurance to last until the end, along with a sense of humour to cope with all the twists, turns and surprises along the way. Oh yes, I am a *true* 'Survivor' – and I don't need to win a million dollars to prove it!

I am a mum of a child with Asperger Syndrome, all the above, and so much more. Some days I will want to be none of the above – and just be a typical mum with a typical child, doing typical things. On those days I will know it's OK to be angry, and to cry, and to lean on my family, friends, and church for support.

Because after all, the most important thing I am, is human.

And on this day, and any other day I need to, I will read this as a reminder, of just who it is, I am…

'I am...' a piece of creative writing by Michelle Guppy of TX, USA. Michelle was the force behind the widely successful 2000 Autism Awareness Rally held in Washington DC. 'I am...' touches all mothers of children with Asperger Syndrome. (For this publication the word 'Autism' has been replaced with 'Asperger Syndrome'.)